# Cultural Traditions in

# India

Molly
Aloian

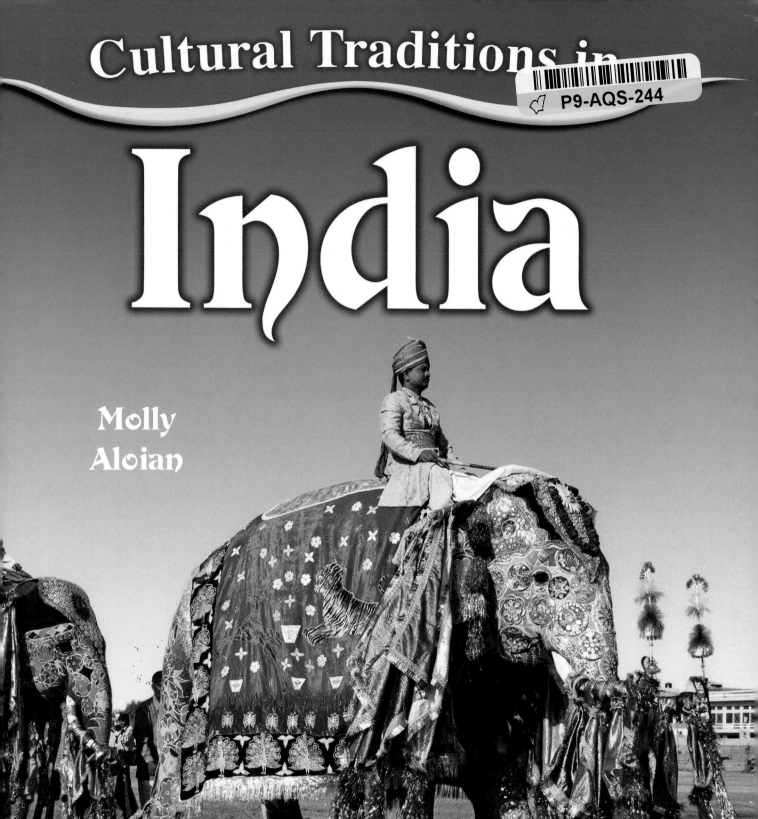

Crabtree Publishing Company

www.crabtreebooks.com

# Crabtree Publishing Company

## www.crabtreebooks.com

**Author:** Molly Aloian
**Publishing plan research and development:**
 Sean Charlebois, Reagan Miller
 Crabtree Publishing Company
**Project coordinator:** Kathy Middleton
**Editor:** Kathy Middleton
**Proofreader:** Crystal Sikkens
**Photo research:** Allison Napier, Crystal Sikkens
**Design:** Katherine Berti
**Production and print coordinator:** Katherine Berti
**Prepress technician:** Katherine Berti

**Cover:** Indian sweets known as mithai (top right); mendhi tattoos made from henna ink (top left); young woman at Holi festival (middle center); Indian dancer performing classical dance (middle right); annual elephant festival in Jaipur, India (middle left); Diwali lamps (bottom center); fireworks during Diwali (background)
**Title page:** Annual elephant festival in Jaipur, India

**Photographs:**
Associated Press: Bikas Das: page 15 (bottom)
BigStockPhoto: Archana Bhartia: front cover (top left)
Dreamstime: Sunil281: front cover (top right); Samrat35: pages 7 (top), 12, 13 (bottom); Angela Ostafichuk: page 7 (bottom); Nantucket photo art: page 11; Percom: page 21 (top); Reddees: page 23 (right)
iStockphoto: thefinalmiracle: front cover (background)
Keystone Press: © Stringer/zumapress: page 25
Shutterstock: Dana Ward: front cover (middle center); Alfred Wekelo: front cover (middle right); Jeremy Richards: front cover (middle left), pages 1, 9; dp Photography: page 4; VLADJ55: page 5; AJP: page 6; Aleksandar Todorovic: page 13 (top); Avik: page 14; Angelo Glampiccolo: page 16; doonbugsbunny: pages 18, 19 (top); neelsky: page 23 (left); Paul Prescott: page 24; Malgorzata Kistryn: page 27 (top)
Wikimedia Commons: page 28; Antônio Milena: page 8; Thamizhpparithi Maari: page 10 (top); Bpilgrim: page 15 (top); Capt. Saravanan: page 17; Manoj Vishvakarma: page 19 (bottom); Nimitnigam: pages 20–21; Kalakki: page 22; Subharnab Majumdar: page 26 (top); Arne Hückelheim: pages 26-27; Giridhar Appaji Nag Y: page 29; Amartyabag: page 30; Shantanu Adhicary: page 31

**Library and Archives Canada Cataloguing in Publication**

Aloian, Molly
 Cultural traditions in India / Molly Aloian.

(Cultural traditions in my world)
Includes index.
Issued also in electronic format.
ISBN 978-0-7787-7585-0 (bound).--ISBN 978-0-7787-7592-8 (pbk.)

 1. Festivals--India--Juvenile literature. 2. Holidays--India--Juvenile literature. 3. India--Social life and customs--Juvenile literature. I. Title. II. Series: Cultural traditions in my world

GT4876.A2A56 2012      j394.26954      C2012-900866-4

**Library of Congress Cataloging-in-Publication Data**

Aloian, Molly.
Cultural traditions in India / Molly Aloian.
 p. cm. -- (Cultural traditions in my world)
Includes index.
ISBN 978-0-7787-7585-0 (reinforced library binding : alk. paper) -- ISBN 978-0-7787-7592-8 (pbk. : alk. paper) -- ISBN 978-1-4271-7864-0 (electronic pdf) -- ISBN 978-1-4271-7979-1 (electronic html)
 1. Holidays--India--Juvenile literature. 2. Festivals--India--Juvenile literature. 3. India--Social life and customs--Juvenile literature. I. Title.

GT4876.A2 A67 2012
394.26954--dc23

              2012004029

## Crabtree Publishing Company

www.crabtreebooks.com      1-800-387-7650

Printed in the U.S.A./032012/CJ20120215

Copyright © **2012 CRABTREE PUBLISHING COMPANY.** All rights reserved. No part of this publication may be reproduced, stored in a retrieval system or be transmitted in any form or by any means, electronic, mechanical, photocopying, recording, or otherwise, without the prior written permission of Crabtree Publishing Company. In Canada: We acknowledge the financial support of the Government of Canada through the Canada Book Fund for our publishing activities.

**Published in Canada**
Crabtree Publishing
616 Welland Ave.
St. Catharines, ON
L2M 5V6

**Published in the United States**
Crabtree Publishing
PMB 59051
350 Fifth Avenue, 59th Floor
New York, New York 10118

**Published in the United Kingdom**
Crabtree Publishing
Maritime House
Basin Road North, Hove
BN41 1WR

**Published in Australia**
Crabtree Publishing
3 Charles Street
Coburg North
VIC 3058

# Contents

# Welcome to India

India is a country in South Asia. With over one billion people it is the second-largest country in the world. Its famous landforms, such as the Himalaya Mountains, the Thar Desert, and the Ganges River, have inspired India's people and helped shape their customs and traditions for thousands of years.

**Did you Know?**
India's capital city is New Delhi. Over 21 million people live in New Delhi.

This book highlights many of the holidays, festivals, traditions, and customs that Indians celebrate throughout the year. India's people are a diverse mix of ethnic groups speaking over 200 languages. Many of India's holidays are based on Hinduism. There are also several national holidays celebrating India's independence as a country.

Of course, Indians also celebrate personal events, such as birthdays and weddings, throughout the year.

About 80 percent of the population of India follows the Hindu religion. Many bright and colorful Hindu temples can be seen throughout India.

# New Year

New Year's Day is celebrated at different times of the year in different parts of India. Many people throughout India follow the Gregorian calendar, which is the same one used in North America. New Year's Day is celebrated with friends and family on January 1. Exchanging greeting cards and small gifts is often part of the New Year's Day celebrations in India.

People are shown performing traditional dances on New Year's Day in Kerala.

These people are participating in a special street parade in West Bengal.

Bollywood is the nickname for the Indian film industry. Bollywood produces over 800 movies per year.

Larger cities, including Mumbai, New Delhi, Bangalore, and Chennai, organize live concerts, which are attended by Bollywood stars and other well-known people in India. The concerts attract large crowds of people. There is singing, dancing, music, and fireworks.

# Republic Day

Republic Day is one of three national holidays in India. January 26 marks the day in 1950 that India became a **republic**. Republic Day is celebrated all over the country and especially in India's capital, New Delhi.

**Did you Know?**
Republic Day is one of the most popular holidays in India.

Camel-mounted police ride as part of the Republic Day parade in New Delhi.

The Indian Army's motorbike display team is also part of the Republic Day parade.

On Republic Day, there is a huge parade in New Delhi. Members of the Indian army, navy, and air force march in their military uniforms. Cadets and school children consider it a great honor to participate in this event. There are also colorful floats representing the different states of India. Each float is meant to show the **diversity** and richness of the culture of India.

# Pongal

People living in the southern part of India celebrate Pongal in January. Pongal is a harvest festival that starts on January 14 of each year. The celebration usually lasts for three or four days. During this time, people clean their houses, wear new clothes, and most importantly, give thanks for the rice harvest.

Pongal is named after a sweet rice pudding called pongal.

**Did you Know?** Cattle are **sacred** to Hindus. During Pongal, people put flower garlands on cattle as a sign of honor and respect.

On the first day of the festival, people offer pongal to the rain gods to say thank you for providing rain for the rice harvest. On the second day, people offer pongal to the sun god named Surya for helping to ripen the rice. On the third day, people clean their cattle and decorate the cattle with flowers, bells, and colored powders. They are honoring the cattle for plowing the fields for the harvest.

These dancers are celebrating Pongal in South India.

# Holi

Hindus celebrate Holi on the day after the full moon in February or March. During the festival, Hindus celebrate the beginning of spring. They also honor and remember important events in Hindu **mythology** in which forces of good overcame forces of evil.

**Did you Know?**
Traditionally, people celebrated Holi for five days. Today, most people celebrate Holi for two or three days.

University students in Kolkata sing and dance during the Holi festival.

People have been celebrating Holi since ancient times, but it is one of the least religious Hindu holidays. It is a time for Hindus to relax and have fun. People light huge bonfires, sing, and dance. Throwing colored powder and water is another Holi tradition. People throw and smear the powder on one another until they are completely covered in green, yellow, blue, and red powders.

These students are smearing purple and red powders on each other to celebrate Holi.

# Buddha Purnima

This metal statue of a preaching Buddha is in a monastery in Chandragiri.

Buddha Purnima, or Vesak, is one of the most sacred holy days in Buddhism. It marks the anniversary of the Buddha's birth, **enlightenment**, and death. The exact date varies, but the celebrations usually take place in April or May.

**Did you Know?**
The Buddha's mother is said to have given birth to him in a garden in the foothills of the Himalaya Mountains while on the way to her parents' home.

The Buddha is said to have reached enlightenment here at the Mahabodhi Temple.

People bring flowers and offerings to temples during Buddha Purnima. They clean the temples and decorate them with lights and lanterns. They also listen to special talks on the life of the Buddha. Prayers, sermons, recitations of the scriptures, and **processions** are also part of Buddha Purnima celebrations.

These women are placing garlands on a statue of the Buddha during Buddha Purnima.

# Independence Day

People celebrate Independence Day on August 15 each year. It is a national holiday in India, and marks the day that India became an independent country in 1947. There are flag-raising ceremonies all over the country on Independence Day, but the main event takes place in Delhi. The Prime Minister raises the national flag at the Red Fort and gives a speech.

The Red Fort was built as the palace for the Mughal emperor Shah Jahan. Its gigantic walls are made out of red sandstone.

On Independence Day, people also honor and remember the leaders and other people who fought for India's independence from Great Britain. Many people spend the day flying kites, having picnics, and singing songs.

Students do not go to classes on Independence Day. They gather at their school to raise the flag and sing the national anthem.

# Raksha Bandhan

Raksha Bandhan, or Rakhi, is a festival that celebrates and honors the bond between sisters and brothers. People in India celebrate this festival on the full moon in the month of August. During the festival, a sister ties a sacred thread, called a rakhi, around her brother's wrist. The rakhi is considered a symbol of protection. It is believed that the brother must then protect his sister with his life.

**Did you Know?**
A rakhi is made of interwoven red and gold threads. It is believed to provide protection for one year.

Brothers often give their sisters gifts or money on Rakhi and promise to help and protect them.

Today, other people besides brothers and sisters can participate in Raksha Bandhan. Rakhis are often shared between close friends. Priests tie rakhis around the wrists of members of the church. Women tie rakhis around the wrist of the prime minister. Rakhis are also tied around the wrists of soldiers.

This girl is tying a rakhi on her mother's wrist.

# Eid al-Fitr

Muslims celebrate Eid al-Fitr at the end of Ramadan. Ramadan is a month-long Muslim holiday that takes place in the ninth month of the lunar calendar. Eid al-Fitr is a joyous three-day celebration. People celebrate with friends and family. Festive lights, games, new clothing, toys, and fireworks are all part of the fun of Eid al-Fitr.

Thousands of Muslims gather at the largest mosque in India, Jama Masjid, to perform the Eid prayer on the morning of Eid al-Fitr.

During Eid al-Fitr, Muslims end their fast. People share food such as dates and rice. Families also eat meats such as spicy chicken, beef, or lamb. Many people celebrate in their homes, but there are also celebrations at mosques, parks, community centers, family fun centers, and restaurants.

Young Indian girls often apply *Mehndi*, or henna designs, to their hands and feet on Eid al-Fitr and people wish others *Eid Mubarak*, meaning blessed festival. This is the traditional Eid al-Fitr greeting, which is often followed by a hug.

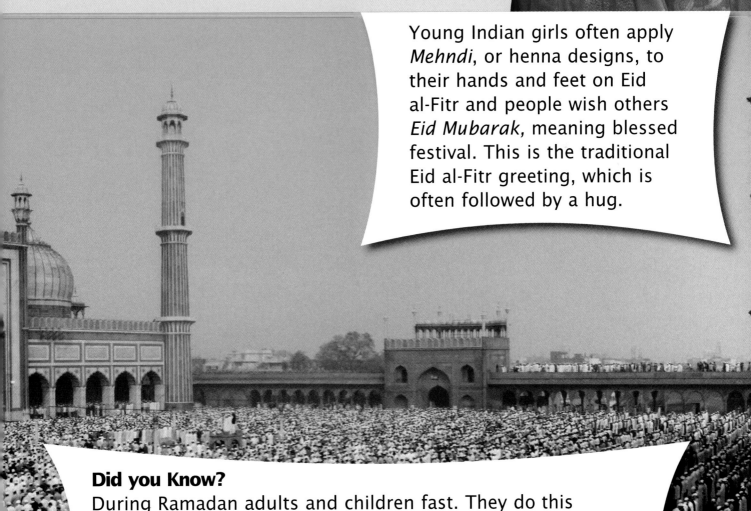

**Did you Know?**
During Ramadan adults and children fast. They do this to purify, or clean, themselves. They also fast to remind themselves of people who are less fortunate than themselves.

# Ganesh Chaturthi

People in India celebrate Ganesh Chaturthi, which is the birthday of Ganesha, the elephant god. The festival is especially important in the state of Maharashtra, where it was first celebrated. Ganesha is the Hindu god of success and the destroyer of evils and obstacles. He is also honored as the god of education, knowledge, wisdom, and wealth.

**Did you Know?** Ganesh Chaturthi usually takes place in mid-August or mid-September and lasts for ten days.

To celebrate this festival, people make clay models of Ganesha. They place the models in their homes or in outdoor tents for people to view and worship. People offer coconuts, flowers, and **camphor** to Ganesha. On the last day of the festival, people take their models through the streets, singing and dancing in a procession. Ganesha is then immersed in water. This symbolizes the washing away of all misfortunes and obstacles.

This potter has created a large clay model of Ganesha.

This Ganesha statue is immersed in water on the last day of Chaturthi.

# Gandhi Jayanti

In India, Gandhi Jayanti is a national holiday that is celebrated on October 2 each year. This date is the birthday of the famous political and spiritual leader named Mohandas Gandhi. In India, Gandhi is known as "The Father of the Nation." He was born on October 2, 1869.

**Did you Know?**
In 2007, the United Nations declared October 2 the International Day of Non-Violence.

This large statue of Gandhi is in New Delhi.

Gandhi believed in non-violent resistance, and tried hard to improve life for the poorest people in India. He encouraged Indian people of different religions to live in harmony with one another and tolerate one another's differences. Instead of violent protests, Gandhi fasted in protest. He also led peaceful marches. He used these methods of non-violence to help lead India toward independence from Great Britain in 1947.

India's prime minister is shown here honoring Gandhi's memory in New Delhi.

# Diwali

The four-day festival of Diwali, or Deepavali, is commonly referred to as the "Festival of Lights." During Diwali, people celebrate the victory of good over evil, purity over impurity, and light over darkness. People light rows of clay lamps or hang strings of electric lights outside their homes. People believe this symbolizes the inner light that protects them.

People make decorative designs on the floors of their living rooms during Diwali. The designs are meant to welcome Hindu gods and goddesses.

**Did you Know?**
Diwali began as a harvest festival that marked the last harvest of the year before winter. It is usually celebrated in October or November.

Fireworks, bonfires, flowers, and sharing treats with family members are all part of Diwali. People also worship the Hindu goddess of wealth named Lakshmi. In fact, some people believe that Lakshmi wanders the Earth looking for homes where she will be welcomed. People open their doors and windows and light lamps to welcome Lakshmi into their homes.

This photo shows Lakshmi sitting on a red lotus flower, a symbol of love and compassion.

27

# Guru Nanak Jayanti

Guru Nanak Jayanti is a festival that celebrates the birth of Guru Nanak. He is the founder of a type of religion called Sikhism. Guru Nanak was born in 1469 in what is now Pakistan. People usually celebrate this festival in November.

Guru Nanak is in the center of this 19th century painting.

**Did you Know?**
During Guru Nanak Jayanti, Sikhs sing, pray, and eat together. Sikhs pray at places called Gurdwaras. They decorate the Gurdwaras with flowers, lights, and flags.

The Akal Takht, a meeting place of the Sikh religion, is lit up for Guru Nanak Jayanti.

Sikhs celebrate Guru Nanak Jayanti by reading the Sikh holy book, which is called the Guru Granth Sahib. They read it continuously from beginning to end. This is done by a team of Sikh men and women, reading for 2–3 hours each, beginning two days before, and ending early on the morning of, Guru Nanak's birthday.

# Christmas

In India, most of the population is Hindu or Muslim, but there are millions of Christians that live in India. Long ago, British **colonists** introduced the people of India to the tradition of celebrating Christmas. Christians in India celebrate Christmas on December 25 each year.

Like in North America, many people in India decorate for Christmas with colored lights, balls, bells, and stars.

Many people attend a midnight mass at church on Christmas Eve. Churches are decorated with poinsettia flowers and candles. After midnight mass, many people go home to a feast of various types of **curries**.

**Did you Know?** In some parts of India people decorate mango or banana trees for Christmas.

St. George's Cathedral, shown here, is in the center of the city of Chennai.

# Glossary

**camphor** A tough, gummy substance that comes from the bark of the camphor tree

**colonists** People who take part in establishing new territories

**curry** Foods seasoned with curry powder, or ground spices

**diversity** Describing people or things that are different from one another

**enlightenment** Obtaining knowledge or understanding

**lunar calendar** A calendar based on the phases of the Moon

**mythology** A collection of stories that deal with the gods, goddesses, and heroes of a particular group of people

**processions** Groups of people moving along in an orderly way

**republic** A type of government that allows its citizens to vote

**sacred** Describing something that deserves respect and honor

# Index